THE
NORTHBAY
SAVINGS BANK
COLLECTION

The Northbay Savings Bank Collection

Artist
Dick Shell

Text by
Ed Mannion

Edited by
Adam R. Collings

Project Co-ordinator
Jeanne Chalmers

Mechanical Production
David Brzowski

Arrowhead Mountain

B O O K S

Published in the United States
by

ADAM RANDOLPH COLLINGS
incorporated

Box 8658 · Holiday Station
Anaheim · California · 92812

Library of Congress
Catalog Card Number 90-93066

ABOUT THE ARTIST

Richard J. Shell was born and raised in Petaluma. He studied at the Academy of Advertising Art in San Francisco and later at San Francisco State College, then travelled to New York City, where he completed a Master's Degree at Columbia University in 1950. Dick's student days were interrupted twice for service in the Navy, first during World War II and later in Korea. In 1950 Dick settled in Denver, Colorado, where he stayed until 1968.

Most of Dick's major exhibits and commissions have been executed in the watercolor medium, using either conventional or acrylic watercolors, although he has worked in many mediums. His love of watercolors stems from his early study with Dong Kingman and the Japanese artist, Mikomi.

During his time in Denver, Dick held important one-man shows at such prestigious locations as the Denver Art Museum and the DeYoung Museum in San Francisco. He also exhibited widely in group shows throughout the country and won numerous awards. This led to his association with Mr. Lemon Saks, who became his agent and continued in that capacity for twenty-five years, from 1953 to 1978.

Mr. Saks had three galleries in Colorado, one each in Tulsa and Dallas, and exchange arrangements with galleries in New York, Chicago, and San Francisco as well. Therefore, Dick's work was displayed over a wide area. In addition to his gallery work while he was in Denver, Dick executed a number of commissioned assignments, including some for Allstate Insurance, Sundstrand Aviation, Martin Marietta, CF & I Steel, and numerous ski areas throughout the country. His waterfall scenes for Coors Beer appeared on billboards and in magazine ads throughout the West, paintings which became probably his best known work of this type.

In 1968 Dick moved back to New York City, where he continued to paint and to exhibit, not only for Saks' Galleries, but at the Lord and Taylor Gallery and the Park South Gallery, both in New York City, and at the Mikelson Gallery in Washington, D.C. In addition, he did many book covers and illustrational assignments for publishers including Dodd & Mead, Charles Scribners, American Book Co., and Atheneum Press, and numerous advertising agencies as well. Shell's work has been

published in *Life, Time, Fortune,* skiing magazines, and many regional and trade publications.

A series of six scenes each of historic Williamsburg, Washington, D.C., Philadelphia, Boston, and New York was the most satisfying assignment Dick received during his New York period. The scenes from these East Coast cities were published by the Donald Art Print Company as prints, cards, and calendars.

In the early 1970s, Dick accepted a job playing the violin and viola with a Mexican symphony. From Mexico he sent many paintings back to Mr. Saks in Colorado, and he also exhibited with the Misrachi Gallery in Mexico City.

Upon his return to the States, Mr. Shell settled in Scottsdale, Arizona, to pursue the challenge of painting desert scenes. There he taught for five years at the Maricopa County Community College. His ambitions in the Southwest were interrupted, however, when Western Federal Savings of Colorado asked him to paint a series of paintings showing "Historic Mansions" built in Colorado by the silver barons before the turn of the century. Three years and fifty-four paintings later, all were on permanent display throughout Western Federal's twenty-two branches and at the Colorado State Historical Society. So much for painting the desert!

In late 1978, Dick returned to his hometown of Petaluma to care for his ailing mother, who was then eighty-eight years old. A well-known local school teacher, Mrs. Hazel C. Shell passed away in 1979.

The artist Dick Shell is also a violinist, and a violinist who wanted a pianist to accompany him in playing sonatas. That is how he met Jean Holm, a well-known Petaluma pianist and piano teacher since 1946. The sonatas went very well and they were married in 1980. At the present, Dick is still painting, of course, and he exhibits in several local galleries in this area.

To create this collection of historic scenes in and around Sonoma County has been his most exciting challenge, and it has brought tremendous satisfaction both to the artist and to his newest benefactor, Northbay Savings Bank, and to the community as a whole as well.

7

ABOUT THE AUTHOR

"President of Petaluma River" is the title, set in large type, on Ed Mannion's unusual business card, which designates the bearer as follows: "Regional History Buff, Bottle Collector, Old Postcard Enthusiast, Local Relic Hunter."

Mannion was born in Nebraska and raised in Iowa. He first saw Petaluma River from the window of a troop train during World War II. His destination was Two Rock Ranch Station, where he and other members of the 112th Radio Intelligence Company studied Japanese code before leaving for the South Pacific. They accomplished their motto, "Home and Alive by 1945," and sailed back under the Golden Gate Bridge in late December of that year.

A graduate of the University of Iowa in journalism, Ed edited a publication called "The Williwaws" for the Navy at Kodiak, Alaska, while still a civilian. He also served as associate editor of the Army's "Kodiak Bear." A book called "War Discovers Alaska" devoted chapters to both "The Williwaws" and to the "Bear," and both were mentioned in *Life* magazine. While at Kodiak, he helped start a 15-watt radio station and wrote scripts for it. This station proved to be the beginning of what became the world-wide Armed Services Radio Network. During the war, when opportunities allowed he published a small company newspaper called "Snafu," which received mention in *Time* magazine.

Ed met Urla Christie, "Chris," in Aurora, Missouri, where both were students at a photographic and engraving school. They were married in 1947 and eventually had seven children. (Chris died in 1971.) Both Ed and Chris loved to travel, and they worked on newspapers in photography, news, and composing departments, from Iowa to Oregon and from Texas to Alaska. Always in the back of Ed's mind was a desire to finally settle

down in the north bay area at the proper time, that is, when they had so many children that they could no longer travel. In 1952 they moved from Woodland to Petaluma and paid $25 down to purchase their first house in McDowell Village!

While working in the composing room of the *Argus-Courier* from 1960 to 1964, Ed wrote a column called, "Rear-View Mirror." Of all the community events he has participated in, it is hard to say which has given him the most satisfaction. There was the seven-year battle to stop the PG & E from putting an atomic plant on Bodega Head. In 1960 he helped a group to persuade the city council not to bulldoze Hill Plaza Park for automobile parking. Along with researching paddlewheel boats and scows on Petaluma River, the Petaluma Vallejo Adobe has been another of Ed's pet interests. He has written pamphlets and feature stories on the Adobe, and he helped start the annual Old Adobe Days Fiesta. As a member of the 1976 Bicentennial Committee, Ed researched the history of the El Camino Real Mission Trail and established the fact that Petaluma is on the original El Camino Real or Kings Highway. A proper commemorative mission bell now hangs on the north end of Central Park in downtown Petaluma. In addition, Mr. Mannion has participated in the work on the committee to turn the old Carnegie Library into a local museum.

A special source of satisfaction for Mannion has been the visits from authors and students who drop by his home for help with historical matters. He says that it makes him feel less like a nut for collecting all the things that make his home look like a museum. All he asks is that they phone first and bring a rag with them to dust something.

Introduction

Sonoma County boasts an extremely remarkable and rich historical past, a fact that we at NORTHBAY SAVINGS BANK are very much aware of. In fact, Sonoma County is the only place in our country where Russian fur traders and Spanish colonials came face to face. Sonoma County was also home to the Bear Flag Revolt and California's establishment as an independent republic, a brief independence followed by the arrival of Fremont and California's subsequent acquisition by the United States of America.

It was also here in Sonoma County that emigrants settled and established farms that would set the course for the agricultural expansion of the entire state, for the early settlers soon discovered that California required new and different methods of farming, a discovery that led to extensive experimentation. The most highly acclaimed of these north bay pioneers who sought new and better approaches to farming was Luther Burbank.

The list of past accomplishments in the field of agriculture here is impressive: the poultry industry and the dairy industry have both gained

THE NORTHBAY SAVINGS BANK COLLECTION

world-wide recognition for north bay-bred quality and innovative procedures. In the poultry industry, Byce and his incubator are well-remembered, and the dairy industry in Sonoma County led the nation in developing automation in the milking parlor. In addition, the California wine industry as we know it today had its beginnings in Sonoma County.

To commemorate these milestones, NORTHBAY SAVINGS BANK commissioned artist Dick Shell to produce this magnificent series of paintings. This is our way of saying a hearty "Thank you!" to the many industrious, hard-working pioneers who built this county and to honor the rich heritage they have left us. By telling the fascinating story of our local past through these illustrations, we hope to better preserve our rich legacy.

We proudly present these paintings by Dick for your enjoyment with the sincere hope that you will be reminded again and again of the wonderful groups of rugged independent individuals who crossed the continent, those who sailed around the horn, those who built the railroads and the buildings, and all those who participated in the events depicted herein.

Sincerely,
The Board of Directors of Northbay Savings Bank

VALLEJO'S PETALUMA ADOBE – 1840s

As one of the favorite subjects for both photographers and artists, the Petaluma Vallejo Adobe almost always is depicted either from Casa Grande Road or from the present open end side, looking into the interior of the triangle. This interesting painting is an exception, showing the huge mud brick building as it appeared in the latter 1830s when Indians inhabited a village along Adobe Creek and worked at the rancho headquarters. The youthful Mariano Guadalupe Vallejo was given the title of Commandante-General of the Northern Frontier of Alta California by officials of the Republic of Mexico. His mission was to colonize northern California, stop the Russians at Fort Ross from expanding, and to make friends of war-like Indian tribes. The Old Adobe played a key role in Vallejo's fulfillment of his charge. In 1889, one year before the general's death, Nellie L. Denman wrote him concerning his memories of the local ranch house. She was preparing a talk for the Petaluma Woman's Club. "I made blankets enough to supply over two thousand Indians," came his response, "also carpets and coarse material used by them for their wearing apparel." He went on to tell of a large tannery "where we manufactured shoes for the troops and vaqueros," and of the blacksmith shop which was used "for making saddles, bridles, spurs, and many other things required by the horsemen." Rangers and volunteers of today's Petaluma Adobe State Historic Park keep the legacy of the grand Old Adobe alive.

FORT ROSS

Most Fort Ross paintings show the fort's interior with its chapel as the main feature. This unique 1828 depiction reveals not only the main Russian-American Company complex but also seafaring and daily working elements. Alaskan Aleut Indians have returned from sea otter hunting and head toward shore. On the beach sits a structure devoted to ship building. Four large vessels, as well as barges, sail boats, and row boats, were constructed here where Imperial Russia and Spanish forces circled the globe in opposite directions and met in Sonoma County.

The Russians established Fort Ross in 1812 primarily to supply food for their Alaskan bases further north. Agricultural farms at Bodega, Freestone and the Russian River area didn't live up to expectations however and, as sea otters and fur seals were hunted almost to extinction, Imperial authorities decided to pull out. Captain John A. Sutter purchased most movable property and other assets of the colony in 1841 for $30,000. One of the chapel bells from the fort eventually landed in a San Francisco junk yard where it was picked up by local firemen and used at the East Petaluma Fire Station on railroad property opposite the old Yosemite Hotel. The bell was returned to Fort Ross in 1945 and subsequently destroyed when the chapel at the fort burned. A replica greets visitors today.

PLAZA OF SONOMA

Throughout the years, to paint or write about the pueblo or village or town or city of Sonoma was to feature its extraordinary eight acre-square plaza. The plaza was ten years old in 1845, a year before the Bear Flaggers took over the defenseless Mexican outpost. Lt. Mariano Guadalupe Vallejo, young commander of the Northern Frontier, had marked off boundaries of the large square and surrounding streets with a line and pocket compass. Although his Casa Grande home wasn't finished in 1845, it nevertheless did dominate the north side of the public square. The "Palace," as it sometimes was called, was impressive but not quite as ornate as later artists depicted it. Early residents remembered that holes covered a portion of the plaza as builders used the soil to make adobe bricks. Shortly after Vallejo went to work (with his compass), an observer mentioned seeing animal skulls, mostly cattle, strewn about the place. Another writer noted that wild horses were raced on the square, with bets won and lost. Dog and racoon fights were common. There is no record of California's notorious bull and bear fights taking place here, although they were in fact held later in neighboring San Rafael and Petaluma. The Casa Grande, barracks, mission and church had all witnessed Vallejo's small garrison of troops training on the plaza, but by 1845 the soldiers had been disbanded. A year later the Americans "captured" Sonoma. One pioneer has a recollection of wild ducks spending the winter in the public square. Children still enjoy feeding ducks in what remains the widely-used and historic center of town.

McNEAR'S LANDING

Scow schooners or hay scows once helped Petaluma Creek (now a river) rank as one of the busiest waterways in California. Only the Sacramento and San Joaquin Rivers carried more traffic. Manned by two or three "tule sailors," the small, flat-bottomed freighters could navigate low tides in narrow streams. Delightfully, the Petaluma Transit system uses old schooner names on several of its buses. These are the Alma, 4th of July, Agnes Jones and the Fearless. The Alma, last remaining example of the over 400 schooner fleet which once plied the San Francisco Bay and its tributaries, has since been restored and is today a part of the National Maritime Museum's ship display at San Francisco's Hyde Street Pier. Once a familiar sight on Petaluma River, the Alma returns every year as a feature of the River Festival and Old Adobe celebration.

Towering over the schooner masts at the foot of today's Western Avenue is the 1882 wooden town clock tower, above the iron front Masonic Building. The present copper dome replaced the wooden housing in 1934. Still in operation over the years is the original bell which arrived in town on the Steamer Pilot. Said the local newspaper, the *Argus:* "The town clock is a public necessity. The young want it to tell time to go to school; the old to tell what time to go home. Men want it so they can pawn their watches, and women want it so they can look out their chamber windows and see if their husbands lie when they come home. The clock will not only be a great convenience but will prove a positive conservator of public morals."

21

STEAMER GOLD – PETALUMA

A steamboat named Gold has had a pervasive influence on the local scene since the 1880s. Although there have been dozens of paddlewheel boats throughout the years churning our tidal waters, it is in fact Gold that seems to be indelibly imprinted in most people's memories. Actually, the third steamer to be called Petaluma was more important historically. The last commercial paddlewheeler on the West Coast, it ran a daily schedule (between Petaluma and San Francisco) until August of 1950. Nevertheless the Gold remains the best remembered.

The Petaluma & Santa Rosa Railroad Company, combining railroad and water transportation, often was called the Steamer Gold Line. In the same manner many think of McNear Canal, south of the D Street Bridge, as Steamer Gold Landing. The first of the ubiquitous rear-enders, built in 1883, burned in McNear Canal in 1920. Gold No. 2 continued the popular tradition until dismantled twenty years later. Notice that the old silk mill in the background has only one tower. Once it was the only silk mill west of the state of Michigan. Constructed in 1892, the building was subsequently doubled in size, receiving its second tower some thirty years later. The solid brick plant, at Jefferson and Irwin Streets along Lakeville Highway, is now one of the largest producers of fish line in the country. It once shipped an entire carload of line to a single purchaser–the only such incident in the industry's history.

22

KEYES EMBARCADERO – LOWER TOWN TOMALES

Although depictions of how Tomales looked in the early days are scant, artist Dick Shell has used available records to recreate an accurate picture of the Marin County village, circa 1860. Sailing schooners–and even small steamboats–once reached lower Tomales by way of a tidewater slough known as Keyes Creek. Traces of that waterway can still be seen today, albeit filled in by silting and cut off from Tomales Bay by a railroad bed. Irishman John Keyes, the first settler to make a lasting impression on that part of the county, visited the area in 1849. In the small estuary that today bears his name, he recognized an excellent location for a small shipping port. Keyes and a partner went into the potato business, developing the famous Bodega Reds. They needed a schooner to get their product to San Francisco. The fifteen-ton Spray was the answer to their dilemma. Of course, they transported other products, everything from lumber to an occasional cow or horse. A passenger could board for $8 one way or $15 round trip. Lower Tomales stayed the focal point of local shipping until the advent of the narrow gauge railroad. Starting in 1875, buildings and homes around the now-closed estuary were built closer to the train depot in upper town. A couple of wharf pilings and a metal ring are all that remain of the small but once busy harbor.

PIERCE RANCH – PIERCE POINT IN TOMALES – 1858

Why represent the dairy industry by portraying a ranch on rather remote Pierce Point at the west side of Tomales Bay? The answer is that locale was and is important in an historical, agricultural and certainly in a pictorial way. Pierce Point (called Tomales Point on some maps) was named after a pioneer by the name of Solomon Pierce. He paid $7,000 for 2,200 acres here in 1858. The area, with its singular advantages of feed, climate and water transportation, became the most well-known dairying section on the Pacific Coast. Three generations of the Pierce clan built an immense operation complete with a blacksmith shop, laundry, carpenter shop to make butter boxes, butcher shop, huge barns and so forth. In the yard of the family home was a schoolhouse.

Schooners were used to get produce to market in San Francisco until the North Pacific Coast Railroad reached Marshall on the east side of Tomales Bay in 1875. Even with rail transportation, however, schooners such as the Point Reyes still were necessary to carry produce across the bay. The Point Reyes was a communal effort of bay peninsula ranchers. It had a raised fo'c'sle to ward off waves at the hazardous mouth of Tomales Bay and was powered with a Corliss engine built in Petaluma.

Pierce Point Ranch was sold to the McClures in 1932. Today it is part of Point Reyes National Seashore.

WASHOE CORNERS

A small business community once thrived here at the intersection of Stony Point and Roblar Roads from around 1870 until the turn of the century. Newspapers of that time referred to Washoe Corners as a "village" which included not only the well-known Washoe House but, across the road to the south, a butcher shop, post office, and blacksmith shop.

Why a name connected with Nevada gold and silver mines was placed on the farming face of Sonoma County is not known. Considering its relative remoteness at the time, it also seems strange that so many successful businesses existed here. According to the facts, main travel did not go up the center of the valley during the pioneering days of the County. Marshy lands, especially around today's Cotati and Rohnert Park, made transportation difficult if not impossible during the rainy months of winter. Stony Point Road on the west and Petaluma Hill Road on the east were on higher ground. Notice at that time that the Washoe House had no balcony (as illustrated). It did boast wooden porch awnings on the eastern and southern sides. Built in 1859, the thirteen room, two-story establishment has offered continous service as a roadhouse and hostelry, now well into its second century!

29

POINT REYES STATION

Residents of Point Reyes Station know it is noontime when a device is activated imitating the sound of a mooing cow–a tribute to the area's dairy industry. Historically, a train whistle would be as appropriate since this village began in 1875 when the first locomotive of the narrow gauge North Pacific Coast arrived. At that time the land was owned by Dr. Galen Burdell. It was called Olema Station, but was soon changed to Point Reyes Station. Olema, two miles to the south, had six saloons. A hotel Dr. Burdell built in his town had only one bar–his. Deeds to other lots in his town had a clause forbidding sale of liquor.

The Marin County community was damaged heavily in the 1906 earthquake. With the epicenter a short distance away, the quake pounded Point Reyes Station to the extent that some fences and roads were thrown out of line over twenty feet. Photographs show a locomotive and four coaches pitched over on their sides.

Shocking news of another sort was received years later when Pearl Harbor was bombed. The location of Point Reyes Station near the coast meant military units moving in. A visiting colonel is remembered who enjoyed playing bridge for high stakes in rooms of the Grandi Building. His name was Dwight David Eisenhower.

30

MARSHALL

The little village of Marshall resolutely clings to shore between Highway 1 and Tomales Bay. It has had a colorful and useful past and has a future which is looking up. It was once a viable shipping and rail point for western Marin and Sonoma County farmers and dairymen. Old-timers tell stories of rum-running days when ships with no recognizable names prowled the bay at night. Founding fathers were the Marshall brothers who arrived in 1852. Ten years later they bought 631 acres for $3,816 from Henry W. Halleck. The latter probably is Marin County's most renowned American. General Halleck served as President Lincoln's chief of staff for five years. As a lawyer and banker before the Civil War, Halleck exercised considerable influence on land grant matters and businesses throughout the Bay Area, particularly in and around Marin and Sonoma counties. The Marshall brothers got their land for a low downpayment and monthly payments, this procedure then far ahead of its time. Notice the train of the narrow gauge North Pacific Coast "comin' round the bend." The railroad was the lifeline of many small communities along the line including Taylorville, Jewell's Garcia, Millerton, Fisherman's (Marconi), Hamlet and Ocean Roar. Of these, only durable Marshall has survived.

33

VALLEY FORD

Valley Ford gets its name from a location at the head of tide-water on the Estero Americano. An old Spanish and Indian trail crossed at this point. Interior Indians used the trail two or three times a year not only for gathering shells which they used as currency but for fishing trips and trips for relaxation.

American settlers arrived at Valley Ford in 1849. A small community started near the estero, and with a new post office the place got its official name. Valley Ford remained little more than a spot on the side of the road to Bodega until a locomotive whistle was heard in 1876. Trains had reached Tomales the year before, but a hill of solid rock made the entrance into Sonoma County difficult. A 1,700 foot tunnel is still in existence, though hidden from view of motorists driving directly above it. Also still standing are remnants of the narrow gauge railroad trestle over the estero to the south of Valley Ford. Normally a sleepy hamlet, it received international acclaim in 1976 when free-wheeling artist, Christo Javacheff, hopscotched over the countryside with his famous "Running Fence." Residents said that curiosity seekers brought heavier traffic than the Valley Ford dairy cattle shows of the early 1920s. A couple of exhibit barns from those fairs still stand, as does the Depot Hotel, which today is a restaurant.

34

FREESTONE

Some visitors to the town of Freestone ask if the name has a connection with a peach orchard. It does not. There was a quarry here at one time where interested parties could haul away rock for free. Notice the building at the far end, center, of the picture. Still standing, it was built as a hotel when the railroad came through and is shown in the 1877 Sonoma County Atlas. The entire area retains its 19th century appearance and as such has been zoned as the Freestone Historic District.

Freestone had an interesting beginning. Mariano Guadalupe Vallejo, the youthful commander at Sonoma, was told by the Mexican government to put up a buffer against expansion by the Russians at Fort Ross. He chose three rugged individuals all with the first name of James–James Black, James Dawson and James McIntosh–to aid him in fulfilling this task. Black was given a land grant called the Canada de Jonive situated in Bodega and Analy townships. Dawson and McIntosh went together and applied for the Estero Americano grant. Although Dawson put up the money, McIntosh went to Monterey for confirmation documents. He signed his name only, leaving his partner with no legal claim to the property. As the story is told, the two erected a cabin at Freestone. Dawson learned he was left out in the cold, beat up his former friend, cut the cabin in two with a cross-cut saw and moved his half to another location (sounds like some modern divorces)!

BODEGA CORNERS

This painting shows turn of the century Bodega, known in early accounts as Bodega Corners. It got its name from the port on Bodega Bay. Less known was a shipping point to the east, near the intersection of Bodega Highway and Valley Ford–Freestone Road, on the North Pacific Coast Railroad called Bodega Road or Roads. The town of Bodega, laid out in a triangle of pioneer roads in the 1860s, boasts what may well be one of the most photographed churches in the United States—St. Teresa's Catholic Church, erected in 1867. Another famous local landmark is the Potter School building which gained notoriety from its appearance in Alfred Hitchcock's movie, "The Birds." The old schoolhouse has had an extended life as a restaurant, art and antique gallery, bed and breakfast inn and theater setting.

Juan Francisco de la Bodega discovered the port that today bears his name in 1775, anchoring his little ship, Sonora, inside the landfall that would later bear his name (also called Campbell's Point). When the Russians arrived early in the next century, they built warehouses here and tried their hand at agriculture. They also attempted farming at a settlement called Kuskof in Salmon Valley, just north of the town of Bodega. All of today's Bodega-related landmarks are rich in colorful history.

OCCIDENTAL

Although Occidental lends a special feeling of serendipity to the woods, it has had somewhat of an identity problem. Historian Harry Lapham's research shows that the place was originally named Howards Station from 1876 to 1902. With a change in railroad ownership, the station became Occidental (with a small "Howards" listed above). As if that weren't confusing enough, the community was also referred to as Summit by personnel of the North Pacific Coast Railroad–it was the highest point on the narrow gauge line, 560 feet, between Sausalito to Cazadero–and as Meekers by those who admired Melvin Cyrus Meekers' efforts in helping to build the town. Occidental thrived in the early days as a center for the transport of products to market. Huge saw mills were located nearby. Today, a major seasonal industry is the making of Christmas wreaths. And, of course, there are the Italian restaurants. On Mother's Day it is not unusual for over 6,000 dinners to be served, this in an area of around 800 residents. Calorie Canyon indeed! Featured here in an early 1900s scene is the Altimont Hotel (center) with the ornate Coy's Store next door. The Altimont, built in 1876, was on the site of the well-known Fiori's Restaurant. A change was made in 1989 when the building was remodeled by new owners and the old name used again as Altimont Bar and Grill.

41

DUNCANS MILLS

In a way the railroad depot here is symbolic of the way things have gone in Duncans Mills. They went from good to bad and now are back to happier times. This painting depicts the depot as it appeared shortly after the turn of the century. The town was then a thriving center of commercial activity. The Duncan brothers' sawmill was in operation. The Duncans Mills Land and Lumber Company owned the largest and finest tract of redwood trees in the county. Trains brought a constant influx of tourists. Samuele Duncan started his lumbering career in the Sierra with a partner named Joshua Hendy. They later moved to Salt Point and started a mill. Samuele's brother, Alexander, bought out Hendy and they moved their operation to Bridgehaven on the Russian River. The operation was moved upstream in 1877 to the site which now bears the family name. At one time both narrow and standard gauge rail stock rolled through town. Notice the three rails in the painting. Over the years, with the demise of the lumber industry and railroad traffic, the old station showed effects of ruin and neglect. In first class condition today, Mr. Arnold F. "Swede" Wallen, who has restored many buildings in the locality, has turned the depot into an excellent museum with the help of others interested in the history of railroading. Duncans Mills is a happy place again.

 42

STREET RAILWAY – PETALUMA

Little known to Petalumans today is the fact that their city once boasted a horse-drawn street railway. The Petaluma Street Railroad company, begun in 1889, lasted just over ten years before its franchise was sold to the electric line of the Petaluma & Santa Rosa Railway Company. This horse-transportation system started at the head of F Street next to Sunnyslope, ran up Sixth and Liberty to Western, jogged along Kentucky to Washington, then headed east across the river bridge and railroad tracks to its terminal at Kenilworth Park. A turntable was at the corner of Kentucky and Western. Shown here is one of the cars on Kentucky Street in front of the historic (1870) Petaluma Theater, now the Opera House building. The City Hotel, built in Valparaiso, Chile, and brought to Petaluma during the early 1850s, can be recognized as the building with the turret. The structure later housed the Continental Hotel until it burned to the ground on May 5, 1968. The old City Hall (1887-1955) can also be identified in the illustration at the far end of Kentucky Street.

EAST WASHINGTON STREET – PETALUMA

East Washington Street, circa 1915. An electric trolley of the Petaluma & Santa Rosa Railway Company stands waiting in front of the station at the corner of Copeland and East Washington. Standing across the way by the Yosemite Hotel is a work engine. Up the street towers the main brick building of the Golden Eagle Flour Mill. This stretch of roadway has borne a variety of interesting traffic. In 1880 the thoroughfare was lined with bunting and banners as President Rutherford B. Hayes together with General Tecumseh Sherman and other dignitaries of the day rode in fancy carriages from what is now the Northwestern Pacific station to the fairgrounds, then located on the west side of town rather than at Kenilworth Park. Crowds and flags again lined the street in 1898 when Company C members of the National Guard marched the other way to the trains en route to the Spanish American War (little matter that most of them got no farther away than Oakland). Both World Wars saw celebrations for departing servicemen.

Today the Yosemite Hotel (depicted herein) is gone while the brick buildings of the Golden Eagle Mill have given way to stores of the Golden Eagle Shopping Center. Meanwhile the Petaluma & Santa Rosa Railway Company station has been moved down Copeland Street.

46

MEACHAM RANCH

Liberty Station stood at a "V" point where one railway track headed west to Two Rock and a second struck out for Sebastopol along Pepper Road. The Two Rock branch, with passenger service conducted daily, was in operation from 1913 until 1925. It later provided freight service "by appointment only" until 1952. Tracks of the spur line would be removed in 1953. To the right of the "V" stood the magnificent Victorian home of the Meacham family. In 1985, fire destroyed the house, which at the time was known locally as the Watson place. Other buildings of the original estate, however, do remain and are today a part of the Garden Valley Ranch, located at 498 Pepper Road. Nationally acclaimed for its many varieties of commercially grown roses, Garden Valley Ranch today is a popular site for weddings and receptions.

TWO ROCK

Folks usually are surprised to learn that Two Rock Valley once resounded with the sound of train whistles. News of railroading spread during 1912 when real estate interests predicted a growing community surrounding a proposed terminus at Two Rock along the Petaluma–Bloomfield Road. Although the envisioned "boom" never took place, the rail enterprise did. Beginning in earnest the following year, passenger service continued until 1925. This spur line of the Petaluma & Santa Rosa Railroad then changed from electrical to diesel, with hauls on call until 1952 for special runs of grain, wool, potatoes, chickens and dairy products from the local farms scattered throughout and beyond Two Rock Valley.

Two Rock more properly should be called "Two Rocks." The large twin masses of basalt for which the area is named stand on a hill above the now-silent railroad station. On early maps of the area this place first appeared as Dos Piedras (Spanish for Two Rocks). An ancient trail from the San Rafael mission to the Russian settlement at Fort Ross used the rocks as a landmark. Four large land grants cornered around the natural hilltop "gateposts." These were the Blucher, the Bolsa de Tomales, Laguna de San Antonio and the El Roblar del Miseria. Venerable old stones, these two rocks were familiar sights to Indians and Spanish horsemen long before the railroad entered Two Rock Valley.

STONY POINT QUARRY

Unusual rock formations account for the name of this vast hill country northwest of Petaluma. Located along Peterson Road, off Roblar, west of the Washoe House (see page # 28), Stony Point has provided marble-like stone for local construction of the county courthouse at Santa Rosa. Workers noted the stone, "when being exposed to the atmosphere it gradually hardens until it finally presents a firm surface and when first taken from the quarry is easily worked, being so soft it can even be hewn into convenient shape and form with a common ax."

In 1905 the Petaluma & Santa Rosa Railway Company purchased the Stony Point property and upon it built a siding for easier transport of the rock. News stories of that event report "the easily quarried stone" as being used not only in the construction of the Carnegie Library but in the Phoenix Block on Main Street, in the Miller Block at Main and Washington Streets, in the construction of the Healy home (later the Sorenson Funeral Parlor), the residence of Mrs. Catherine Brown on D Street and in the elegant new Catholic church at Tomales.

The old crushed rock bunkers were dismantled in 1955 when a building for smoking meats was erected on the site.

53

SEBASTOPOL

Although Petaluma always served as nerve center for electrical railroading in Sonoma County, considerable commerce could also be seen in Sebastopol, particularly around 1915.

The building pictured here on the right still stands. It contained the Pacific Gas & Electric Company equipment to step up voltage for the electric rail cars. Present in almost all yard scenes of the Petaluma & Santa Rosa Railway Company were the ubiquitous work engines.

Tracks, first laid in Petaluma in April of 1904, reached Sebastopol in October. Passenger cars were originally painted brown, later white, and finally yellow and red (as seen here). It is said that while white was the most popular color for the cars, so many were mistaken for chicken houses that subsequently innumerable traffic accidents occurred.

Beyond the station at that time was the Analy House, one of Sebastopol's most famous hostelries. The huge township of Analy embraced all of what is today Bloomfield, Sebastopol and Forestville. Jasper O'Farrell, Mexican land grant owner and pioneer surveyor who founded Ranch Annaly (then spelled with two "n's"), is remembered also for having laid out San Francisco's Market Street. Some say that he named his ranch after his sister; others, after an ancient territory in Ireland.

SANTA ROSA COURTHOUSE

Said the sage Plutarch, "So very difficult a matter it is to trace and find out the truth of anything in history." Such most certainly is true even in local matters. Take for instance the name of the wooden goddess that stood atop the ornate courthouse erected on Santa Rosa's downtown plaza back in 1884. Was she Minerva or Juno? Various sources list one or the other with regard to architectural styles. One historian called the courthouse graceful and elegant. Another said its citizens complained it to be neither convenient nor well-constructed. Cost was either $80,000 or $125,000, depending upon the writer. What is known for certain is that it was classic in design and built mostly of stone, brick, and iron. Enormous granite staircases made the entrance impressive, along with the dome which stood 127 feet above street level. Estimates on construction included 800,000 bricks, 240 tons of dressed granite, 137 tons of wrought iron, together with an undetermined amount of lumber and other building materials. The foundation for the courthouse required 21,000 cubic feet of basalt rock. It was the fifth such county courthouse to be constructed. Below the huge dome, with its statue and clock, were four other goddesses dedicated to Justice. Each stood on pediments facing different streets. All collapsed in the earthquake of 1906. Amazingly, no one was killed or reported injured.

SANTA ROSA LIBRARY

Always traditional rivals, Petaluma and Santa Rosa battled over which city would get the most Carnegie money first. The county seat won and managed to hold opening day for its library three months before the Petaluma library cornerstone was laid. Santa Rosa's Free Carnegie Library opened to the public in March of 1904. It was free in more ways than one – all of the money was donated, along with the site and building stones themselves. Andrew Carnegie funded much of the cost ($20,000) with his usual qualification that things went better if the community also contributed. What resulted was a castle-like edifice facing rail-lined Fourth Street. On opening night patrons braved a severe rain and wind storm to inspect main library rooms, space devoted to California, a children's section, and separate ladies' and men's reading rooms (segregation of the sexes reflecting an interesting cultural comment on the times). An account mentions that the building stood firm with "imperishable basalt blocks." Such proved not to be the case, however, when two years later Santa Rosa was shattered by the 1906 earthquake. The library suffered severe damage. Carnegie came through with an additional $6,900 to make repairs.

58

PETALUMA RAILROAD DEPOT

There always was excitement around the Petaluma Depot when a train arrived. This young girl, dressed to the nines, has returned from her first train ride and a trip across San Francisco Bay on a ferryboat. She and her mother boarded rail cars at Sausalito for the journey home. The spanking new depot is shown here in the "teens" as it was built in 1914. Artist Dick Shell, who has illustrated books on railroading for Virginia City's famous railroad authority (including works of writer Lucius Beebe), shows his talent with a jewel of a steam locomotive. Local railroading started here in 1864 on the west side of the river (then a creek) with a small line called the Petaluma & Haystack Railroad, the third rail enterprise in the state. It ran from a depot at the intersection of B and Second Streets to the Haystack Landing about two miles south of town, where passengers and freight met a paddlewheel boat. On August 27, 1866 at the B Street depot the locomotive blew up, killing four and injuring many. Horses and mules were used to pull the cars until the line's demise three years later. By December of 1869 construction of the San Francisco & North Pacific Railway was under way on the east side of the river from Donahue (below Lakeville) to five miles north of Petaluma, eventually reaching Eureka. The SF&NP gave way to the California Northwestern and then to the Northwestern Pacific. At the present time the depot is used mostly as a freight station.

PETALUMA CITY HALL

"Memory is the diary that we all carry with us," wrote Oscar Wilde. Petaluma's "diary" would most certainly include several pages on the old city hall at Kentucky and A Streets and many memories of that building. Although the date on the facade of the historic structure reads 1886, on March 26, 1887 the *Petaluma Weekly Argus* reported, "Our new city hall is nearing completion. It is a very important structure, and when completed will cost the city over $16,000 . . . but few cities in the State can afford so elegant an edifice simply for municipal purposes." Specifications called for two stories with a basement. The latter contained the marshal's office, city jail and room for the fire department. On the first floor were the court chamber and space for the judge and jury. The top floor held the library and public reading rooms, along with city council chambers. Plans called for a large monogram to adorn the face of the building. This monogram now graces council chambers at the new city hall on English Street, rescued in 1955 when the walls came tumbling down. In retrospect, many believe the walls should never have tumbled. Instead of a landmark usable as a community center, the city was left with less than twenty parking spaces. Across A Street (now a parking lot) was a structure used as a pioneer gas station and bus stop. Shown also in this illustration is the Presbyterian Church, located today on B Street, the old library, now a museum, and behind it the Brick School which was dated from 1859 to 1911. Lincoln Primary was built on the site of the Brick School, now the administration building.

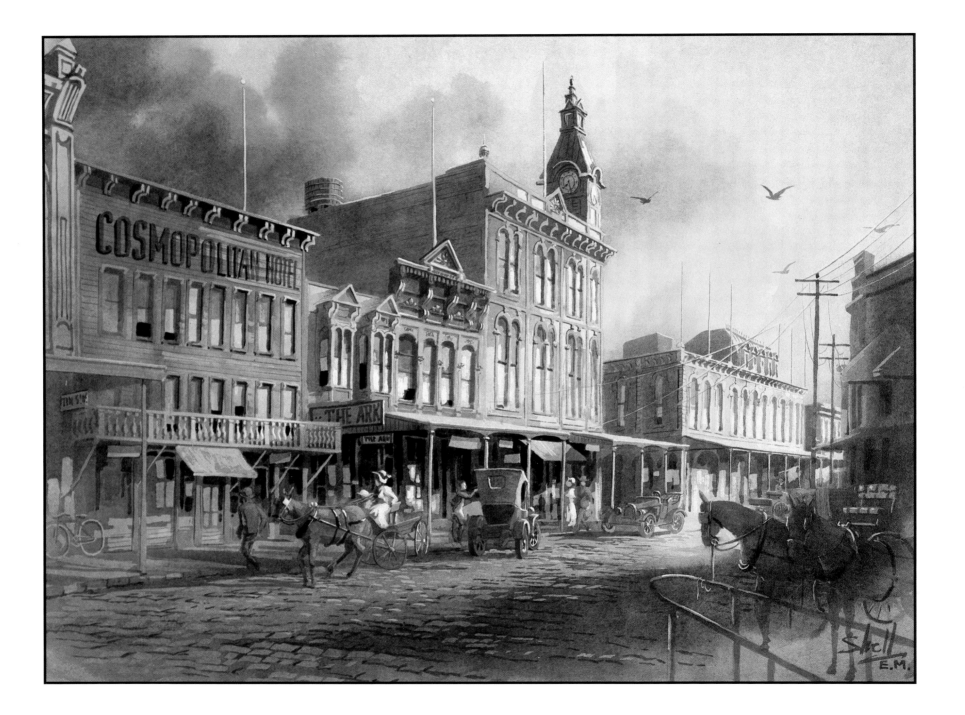

DOWNTOWN PETALUMA

In 1869, when horses instead of automobiles surrounded little Center Park (lower right-hand corner), the hotel shown here was called the Orleans, the next year, the New York. As the Cosmopolitan it stood for decades, until it was demolished and became a parking lot. As such it became famous as the place where youths in the movie "American Graffiti" wrecked a police car. To the north is today's Lan-Mart, which was called the Centennial Block when it was erected in 1876. Construction was started in October of 1875, at which time the *Argus* announced that a new two-story brick building was being raised on the lot between John Pfau's stone stable and the New York Hotel. Thirty-six years later the paper said the livery stable on lower Main Street had closed and that it would seem strange inasmuch as local people had never known the place as anything but a stable. The rambling old brick and stone building, reaching from the present boulevard to Kentucky Street, now contains an interesting shopping center. One of Petaluma's outstanding landmarks, the Masonic building, is next up the line. Constructed in 1882, the style of the three-story edifice has been described as High Victorian Italiante. It anchors a block-long line of cast iron fronts. The Iron Fronts are a rarity in California, as earthquakes have leveled most of them in other cities. Old maps dating back to the 1880s show a grocery store and offices across Western.

IRON FRONT BUILDINGS – PETALUMA

One of Petaluma's unusual titles is "Iron Front Capital of California," or possibly of the West Coast, as only Portland seems to have a comparable number standing. Iron Fronts are buildings with foundry-made facades of cast or sheet iron sections, almost always facing a street, usually covering a brick wall. Different styles of columns, window arches or ornaments could be chosen from a foundry catalog. San Francisco and Santa Rosa had many such structures, but most were destroyed in the 1906 earthquake and fire. Three of Petaluma's ornate and elaborate treasures are shown here along Western Avenue. In fact, Western could be called Iron Front Row, anchored on the west by the three-story Mutual Relief Building erected in 1885. The block-long cast iron fronts are unmatched in West Coast architecture. A horse-drawn water tank wagon crosses the intersection at Kentucky Street, about to pass by the Continental Hotel. This old structure was patterned after an even earlier pioneer holstery called the City Hotel and even used a portion of that structure. The latter was erected in Valparaiso, Chili and moved in 1849 to Vallejo. When that city had a short-lived existence as the state capital, the hotel was brought up the creek to Petaluma. The Continental burned on a Sunday morning, May 5, 1968. In the distance, on the southwest corner of Western and Liberty, can be seen the tower of the Methodist Church South.

PENNGROVE

A poet once wrote: "All, all are gone; The old familiar faces." That isn't entirely true of this painting, as the old Hotel Penngrove building still stands near the railroad intersection. Notice the name Penngrove is spelled two different ways. Originally, the nomenclature was Penn's Grove. One version is that a Mr. Woodward from Pennsylvania named the village. There is a delightful account of how David Wharff, one of the early settlers, arrived in the locality. Said the May 5, 1883 edition of the *Petaluma Argus:* "Mr. Wharff landed here in 1852. He had a wagon and team and all his worldly possessions were in the wagon – including his wife and baby. When they started out from Petaluma his wife inquired anxiously where he was going, and he replied that he was going home. When they reached a point near Penn's Grove–where they now reside–a slight accident happened. They had a coop of chickens fastened upon the back end of the wagon . . . the coop fell off and the chickens all got out–most of them flying up into an oak tree. In reply to his wife, who asked him what he was going to do about it, he said, 'Well, the chickens seem to like this place, and so do I. We are hunting for a home and I think we have found it!' " The San Francisco & North Pacific Railway found the place in 1869. Although the station is gone, freight trains of the Northwestern Pacific still roll through Penngrove's intersection.

69

SANTA ROSA RAILROAD BATTLE

Thunder clouds threatening civil war between two county railroads erupted into a real storm in March of 1905. Battle lines pitted the new electrical road troops of the Petaluma & Santa Rosa Railroad against the older steam forces of the California Northwestern. The focal point was Sebastopol Avenue in Santa Rosa where the P&SR wanted to pass over the CNW tracks into downtown. What followed was a battle royal. Fist fights and rock throwing were minor compared to two CNW locomotives pouring scalding steam and hot water on opposing workmen, a P&SR director throwing himself onto the tracks and almost ending his career forthwith, appeals and injunctions flooding the courts, and photographers and lawyers eagerly gathering. The CNW blinked first. Local merchants and most of the farming community sided with the Petaluma & Santa Rosa juice road whose engines finally crossed the rival's tracks. Santa Rosa's Fourth Street was the main thoroughfare for many years and still may claim that honor to some extent. The P&SR put its tracks right down Fourth for over a mile, almost making the Big White electric cars a part of a local railway street system. Shown is the present Northwestern Pacific station, successor to the California Northwestern, now a part of Railroad Square. The station today is surrounded on three sides by restaurants, a hotel, antique shops and other small businesses. In the painting, a lady seems more concerned about her luggage than any fighting going on down the street. First things first.

70

GUERNEVILLE

Trains in Guerneville! Today's youth with little knowledge of the past might give that as much credence as cows in Berkeley. Grandparents remember the Russian River trains with pleasure, especially the excursion trains bringing thousands from the Bay Area and the heat of the Sacramento Valley during summer months. Not so well remembered were the work locomotives and cars loaded with lumber as mills logged out giant redwood trees in the area once known as Big Basin. Then it was Stumptown. Guerneville (outsiders still pronounce it with an "-ey") got its more acceptable name in 1870 honoring lumberman George Guerne. He couldn't have imagined downtown Guerneville following the 1900s. For decades the river length between Rio Nido and Jenner sported resorts, excursions, picnics, and all sorts of water activities. Helping out was an unusual transportation feature–the Triangle Trip. To take the route in its entirety meant starting in San Francisco, riding a ferry to Sausalito and boarding a train for San Rafael. From there the traveler headed for Novato, Petaluma, Santa Rosa and Fulton, where it was necessary to switch gears west to Green Valley near the Russian River to Eaglenest (later Rio Nido) and on to Guerneville, Rio Campo and Monte Rio. Narrow gauge cars were boarded for the southern run to Camp Meeker, Tomales, Pt. Reyes, San Anselmo and on back to Sausalito and the boat ride to San Francisco. All for $2.20!

HEALDSBURG

When Harmon Heald set land aside for a plaza in 1865, he never dreamed that someday Healdsburg residents would stand on the square to watch what probably was the first grand prix automobile race in California. The exciting event took place May 9, 1909. Twelve cars, driven by amateurs and professionals, started from Mendocino Avenue in Santa Rosa on a planned 52-mile run north through Healdsburg to Geyserville and back. Only six finished the course. A young Santa Rosa butcher and amateur mechanic named Ben Noonan came in first, covering the dusty course in the remarkable time of one hour and four minutes. Third place went to Fred Wiseman who two years later became famous pioneering another means of transportation. He flew the first recorded airmail flight sanctioned by a local post office and available to the public, flying between Petaluma and Santa Rosa. In the early auto contest, both Noonan and Wiseman drove Stoddard-Daytons. The painting shows Noonan gunning in the lead past Healdsburg Plaza as Wiseman passes by the old City Hall. In the distance is the Bank of America Building, occupying the site where Heald built a store in 1852. The plaza, landscaped in 1873, still is the central feature of downtown Healdsburg, a focal point of many events and long the scene of civic celebrations.

74

FORESTVILLE

Why is a 1905 wagon full of chairs so prominent in an historic painting of Forestville? Because these are not ordinary chairs, say early Sonoma County historians. This particular wagon may be carrying the last product of a manufacturing enterprise said to have been the county's first. These chairs, much sought after today in antique shops, may not be handsome but are reported to be as nearly indestructible as such an item can be. Made of chestnut or tanoak (the back of alder and fir), these rustic pieces have seats of rawhide strips (interlaced while wet). Sometimes the seating left an imprint, which explains why some people call them Checkerboard Bottom Chairs! Wagon loads of Checkerboard Bottom Chairs were a familiar sight throughout California and Nevada. One report stated that over 400,000 were disposed of between 1850 and the turn of the century. An early price of two dollars per chair eventually reached around five dollars. Tell that to an antique dealer!

It was A.J. Forrester who founded the town of Forestville. The second "r" of his name got lost somewhere along the way. There was a Forestville Station on a spur of the Northwestern Pacific's line to Guerneville and, over the hill to the south, the Petaluma & Santa Rosa electric line reached the town of Forestville in July of 1905. Although the P&SR planned to go to Mendocino County, Forestville remained the terminus. Today, the town thinks of itself as a beginning rather than an ending: Gateway To The Russian River Resort Area.

INCUBATOR SITE – PETALUMA

Little known Martha Street is the steep thoroughfare on the north side of Hill Plaza Park along Petaluma Boulevard North. Adjacent today is a parking lot and store. Missing is an historic plaque. Why should there be a commemorative ornament on this site? Because it was here that the first practical chicken incubator was perfected back in 1879. The invention, the brainchild of a former Canadian named Lyman C. Byce and a local dentist, Isaac Dias, eventually made Petaluma famous throughout the poultry industry. Byce and Dias worked above the William F. Farrell blacksmith shop on what was then North Main Street. Incubators had been around for centuries–the Egyptians had huge ones–but until the Petaluma inventors put their minds together, no one had figured out one necessary ingredient–that of maintaining a constant temperature. The first small octagonal redwood box with four legs and glass doors, through which watchers could see motherless chicks breaking through their shells, started a poultry revolution. Dias subsequently died in a boating accident on the Petaluma River. His name remains an obscure footnote to researchers. The Petaluma Incubator Company proliferated under Byce. It was built across the street from Hill Plaza Park, today a parking lot. The firm was widely publicized, even in motion pictures. Public relations genius H.W. "Bert" Kerrigan would come along in 1918 to promote Petaluma as "The Egg Basket of the World."

SEBASTOPOL APPLE DRYER

One of Sonoma County's most important industries, the scene depicted here shows orchards, an apple dryer, and a farm home and barn in the rolling hills north of Sebastopol. Old brochures circulated by the various county chambers of commerce and special interest farming groups paint the region as a cornucopia of agricultural bliss. It was in fact truth and not an exaggeration. Historically speaking, as well as in the present, this section of California in many ways resembles that fabled "horn of plenty" image. To quote a 1912 report: "In January there are olives. Oranges are ripe in February, and the first large shipments of strawberries go out in March. April has the cherries, and May the apricot and the height of the berry season. June is haying time, and the deciduous fruits make July and August busy months. September and October find grapes and hops ready; November has nuts and apples, and the latter crop fills out the calendar."

This entire region has been apple country and not just in November. There are apple trees planted by the Russians at Fort Ross that still bear fruit. Official figures from the early teens show over 4,000 acres in fruit. Put a modern Ford or Chevy truck in place of the wagon shown in this painting, and one would readily recognize this same scene today.

SEBASTOPOL PARADE

To celebrate the apple harvest, Sebastopol has put on a parade since early in the century. Flags, families sporting their Sunday best, horse-drawn floats, an electric car on the Main Street railway track– Pasadena may have had its flowers, but during its heyday few processions could match Sebastopol's enthusiastic display of apples.

Typical among early floats were that of the elephant (herein depicted), made up entirely of apples, of course.

Amazing exhibits at the annual Gravenstein Apple Show included replicas of phonographs, locomotives, oxen pulling covered wagons, wishing wells, windmills, harps, ferris wheels, grist mills, religious scenes, schools, and local buildings, all constructed with apples.

Seen here on the right is the gone-but-not-forgotten "Kingsburg Building," which began as the offices of Analy Savings Bank and withstood the 1906 earthquake to become headquarters for the Bank of Sonoma County.

Sebastopol itself was founded in 1855 under the name of Pine Grove. During the Crimean War, when the Battle of Sebastopol was well-known throughout the world, two local citizens found themselves in a fist fight. One barricaded himself in a saloon. Someone commented that the place should be called Sebastopol–and so it was, in honor of the incident. Thus another Sonoma County city derived its name from a Russian source.

BURBANK RANCH – SEBASTOPOL

Luther Burbank's home and gardens in Santa Rosa are well known throughout the world. Not so familiar these days, even regionally, are the acres just east of Sebastopol where the famed Wizard of Botany did most of his experimental work. Enthusiasts who are restoring a portion of the original eighteen-acre plot claim that years ago Burbank's Goedridge Experimental Farm was as famous internationally as were Egypt's pyramids. Such was Burbank's acclaim. He called the Sebastopol plot his secret garden. During its first years he arrived daily at 5 a.m. to superintend the work on the hundreds of plant varieties under cultivation. Sonoma County's most well-known citizen, Burbank created at least one original plant variety per month during his working hours. This process of crossing and selecting many times meant almost countless rejections to get one or two desired results. Neighbors used to wonder about huge bonfires used to destroy rejected material–with not a marshmallow or hot dog in sight!

The major project of the Western Sonoma County Historical Society is to preserve what little remains of the gardens. Under discussion are three acres and Burbank's cottage. Petalumans will be interested to know that there is a record of the plant breeder stating his perference to Petaluma over Santa Rosa. Unfortunately, he also recalled that in his youth he worked a short time for a Petaluma nursery, where he claimed that due to poor wages he nearly starved to death!

ONE TREE CHURCH – SANTA ROSA

Sonoma County boasts two of the nation's most unusual churches. One, in Asti, is shaped like a wine barrel. The second, in Santa Rosa, has been made from a single tree (a giant California redwood, of course). The latter, built in the downtown business district in 1874, was moved to Juilliard Park in 1957 because it was in the way of–what else–a parking lot. Money for moving and rehabilitation was raised through community effort. Well-known regionally, the building received national fame through a drawing in Robert Ripley's "Believe It or Not" cartoon series. Ripley, a native of Santa Rosa, put The Church Built From One Tree in the Robert L. Ripley Memorial Museum. Sources say the mighty monarch was born and grew up near Guerneville and yielded 78,000 feet of lumber (with 30 to 40 cords of wood to spare). Has the famous church traveled its last street through the county government center? Maybe not. Off the beaten path on the edge of Juilliard Park (and with little parking space), this symbol of the county's lumbering industry may well be moved again to a more accessible location. Chances are, however, sponsors of any new re-dedication will have to go great lengths to equal the joyous day in 1874 when Baptists and friends celebrated the original opening ceremony.

SONOMA VALLEY – BUENA VISTA WINERY

Agoston Haraszthy, the Hungarian count and wine-maker who built a castle-like home in Sonoma Valley, was larger than life in many ways. Legend and controversy still surround him as historians try to sort out truth from fiction. Just for starters, is he the founder of the state's first winery at Buena Vista, east of the city of Sonoma, and should he be called the "father" of California's wine industry? Recent research casts doubt. But like Capt. John C. Fremont–who wasn't a "pathfinder" but was effective in publicizing western trails–Haraszthy gets full marks for wide-spread promotion of California's wine industry. A sketch in an 1864 *Harper's Weekly* shows the Haraszthy Villa, standing like a neo-classic temple, near the Buena Vista Winery which he and his three sons nurtured into one of the largest agricultural enterprises in the north bay. The Haraszthys proved that excellent grapes could be cultivated without irrigation, a fact that has since greatly influenced both the use and value of northern California hillsides. An 1869 newspaper clipping remarked: "The Buena Vista property was known as 'The Vineyard' at a time when General Vallejo's estate and a few more smaller ranches were about all there was to be found in Sonoma." Another early article claimed that the Haraszthy residence was the finest on the Pacific Coast and one of the finest in the world. The villa or chateau was destroyed by fire, probably in the early 1870s.

HOP KILNS

The advertisement above appeared in the *Sebastopol Times* in 1917. Similar ads were common, as Sonoma County once was one of the largest hop-producing regions in the United States. Hop pickers were wanted especially along the Russian River from Healdsburg to Monte Rio and in the vicinity of Santa Rosa. River bottom soil was the best for the finest type of the product. Grown on trellises, the beer-flavoring hops were stripped from vines, their buds put in large sacks or baskets by intinerant laborers. All this was before picking machines were invented. The process involved weighers loading hops onto an elevator with an endless belt arrangement leading to kiln furnaces, where they were dried and sulphured and delivered to a building for bleaching and allowed to cool, then sent to rooms for pressing and baling. Sonoma County's hop industry endured for eighty years. The end came around the mid-1950s when, with the advent of new processes, the demand for hops decreased and mechanization made it necessary for larger acreage. Today's surviving hop kilns are a fascinating part of the county's historic heritage.

RECREATION ON RUSSIAN RIVER – MONTE RIO

"Going to the river" still means to many Bay Area residents a vacation trip to the Russian River. In the old days–say the teens and 1920s–such summer fun meant enjoying days and nights at Monte Rio. Once the largest community along the recreational waterway stretching from Rio Nido to Jenner, shown here is a night-time scene at Monte Rio. The composition includes river, beach, redwoods, cottages along the hillside, a train, paddlewheel boat and a three-story hotel that later was made into a seven-story hostelry. The hotel claimed that every room was on a ground floor (possible because the floors were constructed against curves facing the hill). With a capacity for 100 guests, the Monte Rio Hotel also boasted the only passenger elevator in the county. The unique lodge was torn down in the mid-1930s.

In Spanish the word "monte" means woods, low land, thicket or grove. Some attribute the name to "mountain," as in Italian. Whatever your translation, there is little doubt that this area continues as a popular place to live and vacation. Monte Rio partisans call it the "Hub of the Russian River." Under a full moon on a warm summer evening, its motto could just as well be "Hub of the Universe."

93

Plates

1. Vallejo's Petaluma Adobe - circa 1840s _____ 15
2. Fort Ross _____ 16
3. Plaza of Sonoma _____ 19
4. McNear's Landing _____ 20
5. Steamer Gold - Petaluma _____ 23
6. Keyes Embarcadero - Lower Town Tomales _____ 24
7. Pierce Ranch - Pierce Point in Tomales - 1858 _____ 27
8. Washoe Corners _____ 28
9. Point Reyes Station _____ 31
10. Marshall _____ 32
11. Valley Ford _____ 35
12. Freestone _____ 36
13. Bodega Corners _____ 39
14. Occidental _____ 40
15. Duncans Mills _____ 43
16. Street Railway - Petaluma _____ 44
17. East Washington Street - Petaluma _____ 47
18. Meacham Ranch _____ 48
19. Two Rock _____ 51
20. Stony Point Quarry _____ 52

21. Sebastopol _____ 55
22. Santa Rosa Courthouse _____ 56
23. Santa Rosa Library _____ 59
24. Petaluma Railroad Depot _____ 60
25. Petaluma City Hall _____ 63
26. Downtown Petaluma _____ 64
27. Iron Front Buildings - Petaluma _____ 67
28. Penngrove _____ 68
29. Santa Rosa Railroad Battle _____ 71
30. Guerneville _____ 72
31. Healdsburg _____ 75
32. Forestville _____ 76
33. Incubator Site - Petaluma _____ 79
34. Sebastopol Apple Dryer _____ 80
35. Sebastopol Parade _____ 83
36. Burbank Ranch - Sebastopol _____ 84
37. One Tree Church - Santa Rosa _____ 87
38. Sonoma Valley - Buena Vista Winery _____ 88
39. Hop Kilns _____ 91
40. Recreation on Russian River - Monte Rio _____ 92

**THE
NORTHBAY
SAVINGS BANK
COLLECTION**

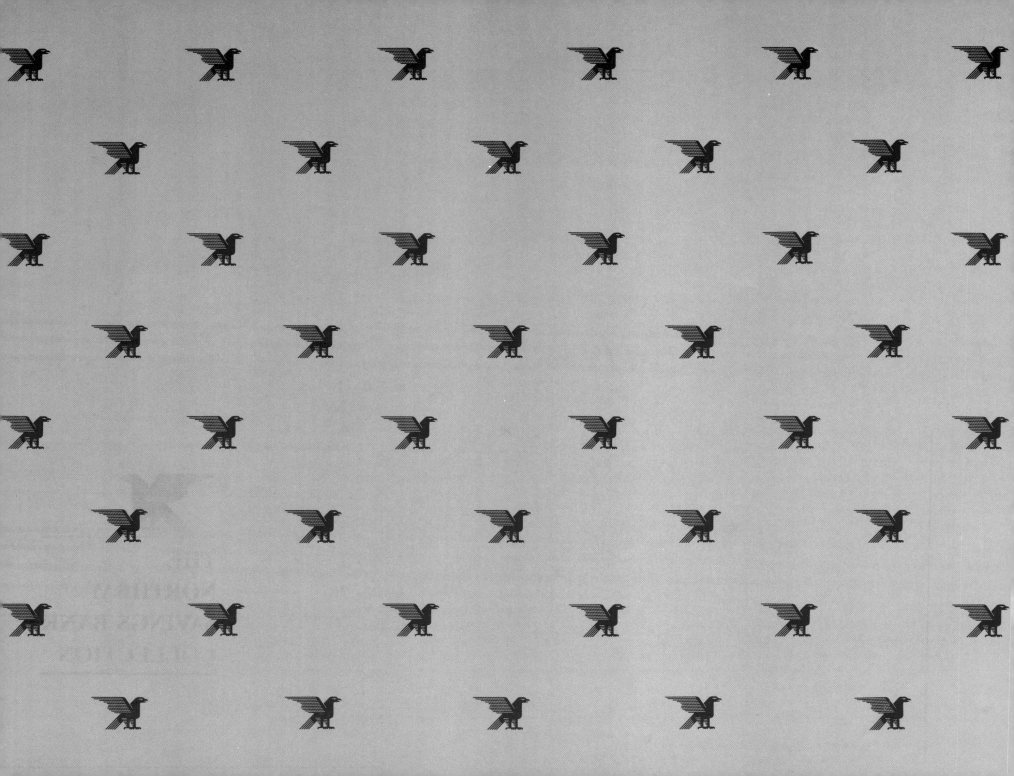